First Easter

Nine Holy Week Dramas

Les Ellison

Nimbus Press
Christian Publisher
of religious drama.

Copyright

We are mainly interested in providing resources for churches that want to use drama in worship, in bible study and in evangelism, and for Amateur Dramatic Groups. You are free to perform any of our plays and sketches and do not need permission but we would appreciate receiving news of any productions. **All our books are protected by copyright and so we ask that you buy copies for each actor when you perform the dramas.** We hope that you will find them useful for the work of the Kingdom.

Fees for performances by professional companies will be subject to negotiation.

Published by Nimbus Press,
18 Guilford Road, Leicester LE2 2RB.
Cover illustration by Darin Mount.

Copyright © Les Ellison, 2000.

British Library Cataloguing in Publication
Data available

ISBN 1874424 52 7

Printed in Great Britain by Moorleys Print & Publishing,
23 Park Road, Ilkeston DE7 5DA, England.

Contents

Based on the thoughts and ideas of John Barton in his book "Love Unknown"

This series of Easter dramas was first performed by the 'Sandon Players' at St Andrews Chelmsford in 1998. Individual pieces were 'Tried & Tested' by 'The Way Out' Theatre Company in Leeds.

Characters

Scene

Christian Drama from Nimbus Press

Various authors

Platform Souls – Gospel Sketches for the New Millennium
(includes a sketch by Les Ellison)
Sketches for Seeker Services 1 – for the unchurched and new Christians
Sketches for Seeker Services 2
Celebrating Light – Sketches for Churches

Stephen Deal

Making Waves – The Quick Sketch Collection
Kingdom Airways – The Quick Sketch Collection 2

Rosi MorganBarry

Angel's Counsel – A True Christmas 'Fairytale'

Ronald Rich

Even More Surprise Sketches
Time to Speak – A play about Peter and Pilate 30 years on

Clifford Sharp (Jonathan Curnow)

The Golden Age – An Environmental play
The Price of Olives – A play about Jesus' family life
My Kind of God - 2 short plays
This is your Life & the Pearl of Great Price
The Good Church Guide – Who's the best?
Looking for a King – 2 new short Christmas plays

Edward Bennett

Lets Go to Bethlehem, Full House in Bethlehem,
Good News in Bethlehem – Christmas plays
The Rose Has Thorns – A play for Easter

First Easter

Nine Holy Week Dramas

The Angels

Junior   *(Silently watching the audience.)*

Senior   *(Enters behind him)* Watchman?

Junior   Ah! *(Turning)* Oh, you startled me.

Senior   I'm sorry. I've been sent to relieve you. How's it going down there?

Junior   Not well. Caiaphas has got all the religious leaders to agree he's a threat.

Senior   Yes. The mediation of priests becomes a little unnecessary when God appears in person.

Junior   He says he's more afraid for the people than for himself.

Senior   Oh, does he? How very noble of him.

Junior   Says: if they proclaim Jesus as Messiah, it could provoke Rome into taking serious action against them.

Senior   The man's no fool. What is he proposing?

Junior   That one man should suffer and die for the people rather than a whole nation be destroyed.

Senior   For once the High Priest and his God seem to have hit on the same idea. If for somewhat different reasons.

Junior	The Passover Feast's only a few days off. If he's going to do something he'll have to do it fast.
Senior	And you can be sure that Caiaphas is as aware of that as we are.
Junior	So it's all going according to plan, then.
Senior	Plan? What plan would this be?
Junior	The Easter plan: Passiontide. Betrayal, crucifixion, resurrection. The start of the whole Christian story.
Senior	I think you're getting a bit ahead of yourself, watchman. These things haven't actually happened yet.
Junior	But they do, I've seen them. And that's only the start of it.
Senior	Such is the privilege of Angels.
Junior	What is?
Senior	To see everything from the standpoint of eternity. To look back to the beginning of time and forward to the ... Well, to look forward.
Junior	But people, the mortals ... They only live in the present.
Senior	Precisely.
Junior	So they've no idea what's going to happen.
Senior	No.
Junior	Ah.
Senior	They haven't decided yet.
Junior	Decided? What is there to decide?

Senior	Their course of action. Their individual course of action which, in turn, will set the course of the next few days.
Junior	But all these things happen, they have no choice.
Senior	They all have a choice. Judas, Caiaphas, Peter. And the names no-one will ever know, let alone remember. They all have a mind of their own. They could choose to act in any of a hundred ways. It's just that we know which way they will choose.
Junior	Except Jesus. He has no choice, does he. He's born to die.
Senior	I think that rather misses the point. He has a message and preaches by God's authority. That will, inevitably, conflict with the authorities of the world. His death is a consequence of that preaching, not the purpose of it.
Junior	What about the Old Testament? All the prophecies? They have to be fulfilled. Everything's laid out for them. They have to follow the prophecies.
Senior	Like some sort of script? With God manipulating them like actors as they play out a tragedy of cosmic significance?
Junior	How else can he be sure of what's going to happen?
Senior	He isn't.
Junior	Are you saying that God's left it all to chance?
Senior	That is his choice.
Junior	That's ridiculous.
Senior	Unless he subjects himself to *all* the randomness and unpredictability of their lives, he will always be a God who has not quite shared their humanity. It has to be all or nothing.

7

Junior   So Jesus might not die?

Senior   No-one who speaks for God, and against the powers of the world, can expect anything else. You've seen eternity. Seen the thousands, millions who will suffer and die just for saying there must be a better way than this.

Junior   So their deaths, and his, are unnecessary?

Senior   Their deaths certainly. As for his, there's at least two millennia worth of argument in that. What is quite definitely necessary, is for those thousands and millions to have a God who knows exactly the pain and suffering of living an uncertain life. Trying to follow his way ...

Junior   Whatever the consequences.

Senior   Very good. But for the moment all *we* can do is wait and watch those who, by choice or by chance, will become involved in the story.

Junior   We? I thought I was relieved?

THE END

The Caterers

Caterer *(Strolling in and answering the ringing telephone.)* Hello? Yes ... Cutting it a bit fine, aren't you? Erm ... Upstairs room okay ...? Good. Nice view. Except it'll be dark of course, so you won't notice really. And you want ... give me that again ... twelve standard Passover suppers. And seats for thirteen ...? Oh. Right. One of you won't be staying to the end. Fine. Oh, hang on a minute, what about wine ...? What d'you mean he usually makes his own ...? Yes, well it better had be a joke. I'll put you down for six of the house red ... Fine. See you later then. Bye, yes. Bye. *(Replaces receiver then calls offstage to his wife)* Hannah!

His wife *(Offstage.)* I'm busy!

Caterer We are now. Get that upstairs room swept. We've got a party in for Passover.

His wife *(Carrying a bowl and some towels.)* Bit last minute, isn't it?

Caterer Yeah, still ...

His wife I thought we were in for a quiet evening. *(She busies herself folding the towels.)*

Caterer That's the thing about this business. *(Sitting back lazily.)* Unpredictable. One minute nothing, the next you're rushed off your feet with not a second to call your own. *(Putting his feet up now.)* Still, it is a living.

His wife Not for much longer if you don't get some work done.

Caterer I am working.

His wife Yes?

Caterer Yes. I'm supervising things. I'm managing.

His wife   You'll be managing to put us out of business if you don't get your sleeves rolled up and wash some of these pots. *(Puts a large metal pot over his head.)*

Caterer   *(Getting up, still with the pot on his head, and talking like a dalek.)* Yes, mistress. We obey. We obey ...

His wife   *(Hits the pot with a kitchen utensil.)* Behave.

Caterer   Ow. *(Removing the pot.)* You could've deafened me. *(Looks at his wife)* I could live with that.

His wife   Passover. *(Working hard.)* Always seems to be a holiday for everybody except us.

Caterer   Don't be ungrateful. It's better than being slaves.

His wife   Really? I hadn't noticed.

Caterer   I mean in Egypt. Slaves in Egypt.

His wife   Oh. Now you're talking ancient history. Well it makes a change from rubbish.

Caterer   It's not *just* ancient history. I mean, God looked after our ancestors then and he looks after us now. Passover helps us remember that.

His wife   Yes? Well what's he doing now?

Caterer   What d'you mean what's he doing now?

His wife   He seems to have turned his back on us lately, what with Romans and everything. We're still slaves. We've just had a change of scenery, that's all.

Caterer   Never mind the Romans, or the Egyptians, or even all the other Jews, all I know is the man what made the universe is looking out for me. His face is turned toward me. And that's all I need to know.

His wife	But you've never seen him, have you? Not face to face.
Caterer	No, of course I haven't. No one's seen God.
His wife	So what's he like then?
Caterer	Who, God?
His wife	Yes. What d'you think he's like?
Caterer	Don't know. Never thought about it, really. He'll have a beard, of course. White probably. Bit unkempt.
His wife	No, I mean what's he like? What is he like?
Caterer	Well ... he's big. Very big. Omnipotent. Wise. Just. Mighty. Not to be messed with, and generally all round ... mysterious.
His wife	Basically mighty and mysterious then.
Caterer	Suppose so.
His wife	So we don't actually know very much about him at all.
Caterer	You're not supposed to know very much about him. Wouldn't be mysterious if you knew very much about him, would he?
His wife	Then maybe that's not what he's like.
Caterer	What?
His wife	Maybe that's what he wants you to suppose he's like. Maybe it's only a PR job. That's the face God wants you to see 'cos he knows you're watching ...

Offstage: the sound of a number of people arriving.

11

Caterer   That'll be the Passover party. *(Moves and shouts off stage.)* Come in, lads. That's it, up the stairs on the right. Yeah, make yourselves comfortable and I'll be with you in a tick.

His wife   ... No. I want to see what God's really like. I want to see God when he thinks no one's looking.

Caterer   I don't understand you sometimes. Here, wash the greenfly off these herbs while I go and get some bread. *(Hands her some herbs and leaves.)*

His wife   *(Calling to him.)* You know what it's like when you're sitting on the bus looking out of the window.

Caterer   *(Calling back.)* Yes, dear.

His wife   Sometimes another bus comes alongside with people looking out of their windows. And suddenly you find yourself looking straight into the face of a total stranger. And for a split second you take them completely by surprise. In that instant you catch them with their guard down and you see them as they really are. Just for an instant. Before they realise you're looking at them and glance away or put up a paper or rub their eyes. That's how I want to see God.

Caterer   *(Coming back with some small loaves and a bottle of wine.)* I don't think God uses the forty-seven bus.

His wife   You know what I mean.

Caterer   How would you recognise him? I mean, just suppose you did find yourself looking into the face of God. How would you know it was him? *(Picks up the basin and jug.)* Pass us that towel. *(Throws towel over one shoulder.)* Sometimes I wonder what you're thinking about. *(He leaves.)*

His wife   If I found myself looking into the face of God, even for a split second, I'd know it was him. I'd know alright. I'd see it in his eyes.

12

And he'd know I'd seen him as he really is. *(Arranges food and wine on tray.)*

Caterer *(Returns without bowl, towel, etc. chuckling to himself.)* Oh, dear, oh, dear.

His wife How are they getting on?

Caterer *(Takes wine and pours himself a glass.)* They're playing, "whose going to wash the feet". They know somebody's got to do it, but no one wants to volunteer.

His wife Why don't they take it in turns.

Caterer Can't do that. That would establish a hierarchy. No, their boss'll sort it out. He'll detail someone to do it.

His wife Which one's he then?

Caterer The one sitting watching their embarrassment, you can't miss him. Take the food up will you? I'll put the kettle on and we'll have a brew.

His wife *(Picks up the tray with bread, wine, etc. and leqves.)*

Caterer Washing feet. Blimey, what an awful job ... Dear, oh, dear. *(Settles himself with the glass of wine.)*

His wife *(Enters with the look of someone who has just looked into the face of God [difficult to act, I know]. She holds a piece of broken bread.)*

Caterer Hannah?

His wife *(Sits. Caterer gets a chair under her just in time.)*

Caterer Hannah? What's the matter?

His wife   I've just looked into the face of God.

Caterer   What ...? Up there?

His wife   Yes.

Caterer   In our room?

His wife   Yes.

Caterer   What's he doing up there?

His wife   Washing their feet.

Caterer   Washing feet?

His wife   Yes.

Caterer   No. Not God, he's like the manager. I mean, he only supervises things. You'd never see God doing anything like that.

His wife   No you wouldn't. Because that's what God does when no one's looking. That's what God is really like. He wasn't expecting to see me. When I walked in he wasn't prepared. He was just ... there. Coat off, sleeves rolled up, towel 'round his waist. On his knees, washing feet. When he looked up, I could see I'd surprised him. I could see it in his eyes. Eyes that see one end of the universe to the other. But in this moment, here and now, just looking at me looking at him. Just me and God.

Caterer   Did he ... say anything?

His wife   What was there to say? He knew I'd seen him.

Caterer   Do they know, the others? I mean that ... God ...

His wife   He's trying to explain it to them. But if they'd just open their eyes they'd see ...

14

Offstage: the sound of one person leaving.

His wife   Someone's leaving.

Caterer   Yeah, obviously doesn't know who he's got up there.

His wife   Oh, he'll know alright. He might not like it, but he'll know.

Caterer   Come on, how can he not like it?

His wife   Well. Washing feet. Not everybody's idea of God, is it?

Caterer   Dunno. It's not for me to go telling God what he should and shouldn't do.

His wife   No. But we all try from time to time.

Caterer   S'pose so.

His wife   Why should God want to get involved with something like washing feet?

Caterer   It's all part of the mystery I expect.

His wife   Or it's all part of the explanation. Sharing our lives so we can share his.

Caterer   Well I can see how he shares *our* lives. But how's he going to share *his* with us?

His wife   *(She shrugs her shoulders, breaks the bread in two and gives half to Caterer.)*

THE END

The Conspirators

Deceiver *(With a fat cigar in one hand, and the other on the shoulder of the Deceived.)* All I'm saying is, with the right manager, the boy could go a long way.

Deceived He walks on water, what could he want with a manager?

Deceiver Hey, hey. Everybody needs a manager. There isn't anything that can't be done better with a manager. So he walks on water. How many turned up to watch?

Deceived Me and the others.

Deceiver Is that all?

Deceived We go everywhere with him.

Deceiver Greatest crowd pulling stunt since Moses split the Red Sea, and how big's the audience? Twelve.

Deceived He gets a crowd when he wants one. Five thousand men, I've seen. Not to mention the women and children.

Deceiver Hey, if you're going to get anywhere in this business, always mention the women and children. They're all 'consumers' every single one. Even our 'mutual friend' knows that.

Deceived I've never heard him call them consumers.

Deceiver Exactly. You see? He's missing the point altogether. Five thousand, you say, maybe more. What an opportunity. He could have sold them anything, and what did he do?

Deceived He talked to them.

Deceiver Talked to them.

Deceived   And he fed them as well.

Deceiver   What all five thousand?

Deceived   Not to mention the women and children.

Deceiver   Well there goes the catering franchise. Pity, I could've worked a really good deal with McDonald's.

Deceived   I don't think he's interested in deals.

Deceiver   That's obvious.

Deceived   What d'you mean?

Deceiver   I mean the way he bust up the Mall in the Temple. Do you know what they were offering for his personal endorsement? He has blown a fortune in sponsorship.

Deceived   Sponsorship? He heals cripples. He doesn't play striker for Newcastle. He makes blind people see, for God's sake!

Deceiver   The principles the same.

Deceived   I don't believe this.

Deceiver   Look, what's the first thing a blind man needs when he gets his sight back?

Deceived   I don't know. *(Sarcastically.)* Sunglasses.

Deceiver   Exactly! So we get Polaroid, Foster Grant, Ray Bann. Hey, how about those reflective ones like for cyclists, You know they wrap around like that La Forge guy on Star Trek. Maybe we can get a TV tie-in, US rights ...

Deceived   He's not interested in ... in ... 'things'. He doesn't own anything. Not sunglasses not anything.

Deceiver   Clothes. He wears clothes. everyone wears clothes.

Deceived   A simple shirt, that's all ...

Deceiver   That's all? Hey, if we get just one designer label on him ...

Deceived   It's homemade.

Deceiver   Trainers. That walking on water stunt's a real shoe seller ...

Deceived   He wears cheap sandals. Look, for the last time he's not interested in promoting anyone else's stuff, he's got his own product, his own line.

Deceiver   And just what is that, huh? What is he promoting? Just what is *his line*? What could be worth passing up a fortune, huh? What could be that good?

Deceived   Eternal life.

Deceiver   Eternal life? Now that's good ... So what's the angle? How's he got it packaged?

Deceived   No angle. Just a personal relationship. With God. Both sides of the grave.

Deceiver   Brilliant. Brill-i-ant.

Deceived   Yes. And you should've thought of it first, Never mind all this marketing crap. Religion's supposed to be your business. Your only business ..

Deceiver   Hey, there's a lot more to religion than simply God, you know.

Deceived   I don't think he'd agree with you.

19

Deceiver   He will when we start working together.

Deceived   What? He's exactly opposed to you. Can't you see that? You want to stand between God and people. He's telling them to deal direct. To cut out the middle man altogether.

Deceiver   *(Thinking of his 10%.)* Can he do that?

Deceived   He calls God his father.

Deceiver   Wow. Wait 'til Advertising Standards get hold of that line.

Deceived   I think it's more than just a line.

Deceiver   *(Thinking quickly and changing tack.)* Look, religion's a cut-throat business. Believe me, I know. It's a jungle out there. There's no room for a freelance like him. I mean, look what happened to that baptist guy. Sooner or later he's got to look for a merger with a big firm. That's us, or the opposition. And you don't want the opposition to get him, do you? Do you?

Deceived   *(Getting confused now, he sighs.)*

Deceiver   No. Look, you know him. Get him to join us. We could use his talent. We've got centuries of experience in this sort of thing. We could mould him, shape him. Smooth off those rough edges. In time he could be something. Part of the establishment. The tradition. You can't beat the tradition.

Deceived   He says he's going to bring it all down and rebuild it again in three days.

Deceiver   There you go, see. More rough edges.

Deceived   He never makes a promise he can't deliver.

Deceiver   And that's just why I've got to meet him.

Deceived   What for?

Deceiver   To test the product. To see if the boy's as good as everyone says he is.

Deceived   He raised Lazarus!

Deceiver   Hey, if he couldn't do stuff like that I wouldn't be interested in the boy at all. No, I want to give him a real test.

Deceived   What've you got in mind?

Deceiver   Don't concern yourself with the details. You just get him here. I'll take care of the rest. And don't worry, I'll see you get properly rewarded.

Deceived   I wasn't worried.

Deceiver   No. Of course you weren't. You just want to do the right thing. Still, righteousness should have its own rewards. *(Counts out a number of bank notes)* Here.

Deceived   I don't think I should ...

Deceiver   Hey, look on it as a consultancy fee. Come on. He'll thank you for it one day. They all will, the whole world. There he goes, they'll say. The man who put Jesus up there where everyone could see him. Come on, if you won't do it for this do it for them. It isn't just for you it's for all mankind, not to mention the women and children.

Deceived   *(He reluctantly takes the money and leaves.)*

Deceiver   You won't regret this, Judas Iscariot. Not for as long as you live.

THE END

The Soldiers

Corporal   *(Getting on with the mundane job of building a full size cross.)*

Private   *(Standing around aimlessly.)* So how many have you done then?

Corporal   *(Without turning)* What? Crosses? Don't know. Hundred, hundred and fifty.

Private   Not crosses, messiahs.

Corporal   Dozen or so. Why?

Private   Just wondered. I've never done any before.

Corporal   Thieves, murderers, messiahs. They're all the same when you bang the nails in.

Private   Yeah. *(With obviously false bravado.)* Bang bang, eh?

Corporal   Yes.

Private   So ... Hundred and fifty then?

Corporal   Something like that.

Private   Hundred and fifty crosses, twelve messiahs. That's about ... one in twelve and a half. Hey, that's pretty good you should do Spot-the-Ball.

Corporal   What? *(Now turning his attention to Private.)*

Private   You know. You have this picture of a football match, a photograph like, only the ball's been painted out and you have to put a cross where it is. And if you get it right, you win a prize. Hey, you could have Spot-the-Messiah. You know, if you get him on your cross you win a prize.

Corporal   Sometimes I get very worried about you.

Private   I wonder what sort of prize you get for crucifying the messiah.

Corporal   Well, if you do get the messiah, I imagine the prize is a lifetime's supply of free electricity delivered all at once in a single bolt of lightning.

Private   Oh. So really, you haven't ever crucified the messiah at all.

Corporal   As I am a corporal engineer in the Army of Occupation and not a small patch of charred earth, I'd say that's pretty obvious.

Private   Rather brings your average down a bit, doesn't it?

Corporal   Just shut up and pass me those nails.

Private   So if this one isn't the messiah either, then we're going to kill an innocent man. And if he really is the messiah, we get zapped by lightning. Don't you think that's all a bit of a waste of time?

Corporal   We're not here to think. We're just here to do as we're told. Now shut up and pass me that nail.

Private   Why?

Corporal   Because if you don't, I'll brain you.

Private   No, I mean why do we just do as we're told?

Corporal   Because we're soldiers.

Private   So?

Corporal   So if we don't the sergeant'll brain both of us.

Private   Oh, yes. *(He quickly surrenders the nail.)* So what makes you think this one's the messiah?

Corporal   I never said I did.

Private   Who does then?

Corporal   They do.

Private   Who's they?

Corporal   The religious authorities.

Private   How do they know?

Corporal   They don't. And they don't care. All they know is he's a trouble maker and they want shut of him.

Private   Why don't they get shut of him?

Corporal   Has anyone ever told you, you ask too many questions for a soldier?

Private   Err ... Don't think so. Why?

Corporal   Look. They can't get rid of him 'cos their religion won't let them. Only the army can have him put to death and the army needs a good a reason. Saying he's the messiah is a good reason. Nail please.

Private   *(Hands him a nail.)* Isn't killing innocent men against their religion?

Corporal   Practically everything's against their religion. They've got more rules and rituals than you can shake an army issue hammer at.

Private   I thought religion was all about understanding God.

Corporal   It was once. But nowadays it's just a checklist of things you do and don't have to do.

Private   And they're not happy with that?

Corporal   They're absolutely thrilled with it. Religion's just like the army. The more rules and regulations you have, the less you have to think for yourself. Gives you a sense of security. No, it's this latest messiah who's not happy about it.

Private   He wants to change the rules?

Corporal   He says there are no rules. Least, none that God's very bothered about.

Private   I'd have thought if God isn't bothered about them, then they can't have much purpose.

Corporal   Exactly.

Private   That'd make life easier.

Corporal   It'd make life unbearable. Religious rules aren't designed to help you understand God, just to stop people understanding each other. They're like army regulations, they keep the insider in and the outsider out. They're exclusive. They mark the boundary.

Private   So this messiah's an outsider then, is he?

Corporal   Well, he's an insider who's taken the side of the outsider. In the army we'd call it treason. Apparently religion isn't any more tolerant and he has to go. Help me stand this up will you?

They erect the cross. There is a nail visible at the top.

Private   What's the nail at the top for?

Corporal   Governor wants to put up a sign.

Private   Sign? Saying what?

Corporal   I don't know, "warning: religion can seriously damage your health", I should think.

Private   Really?

Corporal   No, something to do with his actually being the messiah.

Private   You think this might really be him?

Corporal   I don't know. But even the army can't be wrong every time.

Private   What if he is?

Corporal   Make sure you're standing next to the sergeant. I'd hate to see a perfectly good bolt of lightning wasted on you alone. Come on, it's time we weren't here. (*They collect together their tools and survey their work.*)

Private   If there was no boundaries between people and other people. And no boundaries between people and God. There'd still have to be a point where it all met up, wouldn't there? You know, a place. Or a person. Or an event. Or even a place and a person and an event.

Corporal   I wouldn't know about the mechanics, but it won't be anything to do with this God forsaken place, that's for certain.

Private   No. Hey. We're finished here tomorrow.

Corporal   Yes. Then three days glorious leave.

Private   What's our next roster?

Corporal   Not sure. Sergeant said something about early morning guard duty. In a garden. That'll be nice.

Private   Bit dull.

Corporal   Not if we get to see the sun rise.

Private   Oh, yes.

THE END

The Tourists

Honey (*Dressed as a typical tourist and reading from a guidebook.*) Probably the Salem of Melchizedek, taken by David from the Jebusites, became capital of Judah. Besieged by the Assyrians, destroyed by the Babylonians, rebuilt by Nehemiah ...

Sugar (*Trailing behind her husband. She is a very tired and fed up tourist.*) Oh, Honey. Ain't we seen enough for one day?

Honey This is Jerusalem, cradle of world's greatest cultures.

Sugar These are my shoes; cradle of the world's greatest blisters

Honey Don't you want to see King Solomon's Temple?

Sugar Another piece of kicked about ancient architecture.

Honey It's not a piece of architecture, it's a spiritual experience!

Sugar Has it got a foot spa? We've been walking since sun up and I need a hot shower and a cold beer.

Honey Aw, come on, Sugar. Just the Temple. Then back to the hotel, I promise.

Sugar I ain't going one more step in these shoes.

Honey No need, Sugar Plum, the Temple's right over ... I think we must have made a wrong turn. (*Turning the guide book over and over.*)

Sugar Give me that. (*Takes guidebook.*) Look. We're here: Gol Gotha. And we want to be here.

Honey That ain't the Temple?

Sugar   No, it's a bar. And right now it's the only piece of architecture I want to experience. Ancient or otherwise. And it's about two blocks, so we need a cab ...

Honey   *(Distracted by a distant event.)* Hey, Sugar. Sugar, look. It's one of them ancient cultural ceremonies.

Sugar   It's a heap of sweaty men shouting their heads off.

Honey   Gimme the long lens. Wait 'til the folks back home get a load of this. *(Focussing on the distant event through the telephoto lens of a camera.)* Wow, I bet this is a symbolic ritual that goes back as far as the Exodus.

Sugar   I only want to go back as far as the hotel. That'll do for me.

Honey   There's a couple of guys dressed up as soldiers. Wonder what that symbolises.

Sugar   That they're soldiers?

Honey   And another guy in a long white shirt. Wow! They stripped him naked.

Sugar   Give me that. *(Grabbing the camera and focussing wildly.)* Damn. They've gone and dressed him again. Purple. Oh, Honey. That's just the colour of drapes I've been wanting for the bedroom. We got to ask them where they got that. Now they're putting a spiky crown on his head. Doesn't fit too well. They're having to force it down a little.

Honey   Quick get a few shots. I don't want to miss any of this.

Sugar   Oh, Honey, you know I ain't any use with these things. Here. *(Gives him back the camera.)* Let me know if anyone takes their clothes off again.

Honey	*(Fires off a few frames.)* He's obviously supposed to represent some kind of king. Like the one we saw at the weekend.
Sugar	Oh, yeah. At the street party. Now that little ritual I liked. *(She produces a hip flask, and drinks from it.)* What a parade ...
Honey	Now they're pretending to whip the king.
Sugar	And those dear sweet little donkeys ...
Honey	They are great actors. Look at the pain in that guy's face. You could almost believe this is real. And all that blood. Terrific make-up. Terrific!
Sugar	Palm branches, and people throwing their clothes in front of the donkeys. Honey, if they do that again I'm going to toss that cardigan your sister bought me under those hooves, the orange and mauve one? We'll say it was an accident.
Honey	Now they're bringing in a huge cross thing. It'll be a sort of tree symbol. I guess they're all going to dance around it. You want to see any of this, Sugar?
Sugar	Just let me know when the little donkeys come on. *(drains flask)*
Honey	They're trying to put the tree thing on the king guy's back. It's got to be polystyrene but he makes it look real heavy. *(winces suddenly)* He's gone down. God, I bet that hurt. Can't see what's going on now. *(lowers camera and moves to beside wife)* So much culture. So much history.
Sugar	So what does it mean then?
Honey	Hell! I don't know. Bet most of those guys don't know either. Maybe it's in the guide book. Hey, the king guy's on his feet again. *(Returns to his photography)* Something ain't right here ...
Sugar	*(Flipping through guide book)* It's just a pageant, Honey.

31

Honey	They got some kind of chant going around ... sort of ... Crucify him?
Sugar	Honey, this ain't no pageant. This here's an execution.
Honey	Huh?
Sugar	It's in the guide book, see. Crucify: to put to death. On a cross. What were you saying about culture?
Honey	But why?
Sugar	Why anything? *(Takes camera & views scene.)* Hey, Honey. The king guy. It was him at the weekend. Remember? In the donkey pageant.
Honey	If this is no pageant, then maybe that wasn't either. But they loved him. Didn't they?
Sugar	They sure as hell don't now.
Honey	They made him king. They chose him. And now they're going to ... crucify him?
Sugar	We got to get a new guide book. There's a lot more to this business than crowns and pageants.
Honey	This is crazy. He's their King. They shouldn't be letting this happen to him.
Sugar	It's him that's letting it happen, Honey.
Honey	He's a king. He's supposed to have power.
Sugar	He's got that all right. He's got so much power he ain't afraid of what they're doing to him. Awesome, huh?
Honey	I'm through with sightseeing. I just want to go home.

Sugar   Thought you said it was an experience.

Honey   It makes me sick.

Sugar   Oh, yeah? So what happened to culture? What happened to history?

Honey   It can end here for all I care. Let's go, and hope the goddam place falls down. *(Leaves)*

Sugar   Well if this is the end of history, I sure want to know what they put in its place.

THE END

The Lawyers

Prosecution   *(Triumphantly packing his wig and gown.)*

Defence   *(With a bundle of legal papers tied in ribbon.)* You did it then?

Prosecution   Yes. All indictments proven. Guilty as charged.

Defence   He was innocent. You know there's no doubt about that.

Prosecution   Off the record ...Yes.

Defence   And you feel no guilt yourself?

Prosecution   The beauty of an adversarial system. I won, you lost. Guilt doesn't come into it. *(Smiles.)* What happened in your other cases?

Defence   Common thieves. Legal Aid of course. That'll hardly cover their solicitors time let alone mine. Still, can't blame a man for pleading innocence faced with crucifixion.

Prosecution   Never mind, success isn't everything. Come on. I'll buy you a drink.

Defence   No, no thanks. I think I'll just go home.

Prosecution   Oh, come on now. You're not letting this get to you, are you? One little case lost ...

Defence   Three little cases lost.

Prosecution   Hardly the end of the world, is it?

Defence   I should have only lost two. And I can't help feeling ...

Prosecution   Emotional involvement? Very unprofessional.

Defence	It's not right.
Prosecution	How many of these hopeless cases have you defended this year? One hundred? Two hundred? And how many have you lost? Practically all of them. You can't go wallowing in self pity at losing this one.
Defence	It's not me I feel sorry for ...
Prosecution	Well don't waste your pity on him.
Defence	What, don't pity an innocent man?
Prosecution	Look it was a no-win case from the start. What evidence did he offer in his defence?
Defence	Nothing, he never said a word.
Prosecution	What about witnesses?
Defence	None.
Prosecution	Alibi? Scientific evidence? Character witnesses?
Defence	No.
Prosecution	Exactly. Hopeless. A vagrant, a self-proclaimed leader of a band of ruffians. And a string of minor offences ...
Defence	None of them proven.
Prosecution	And a Northerner. I'm surprised even you would take him on.
Defence	*(Thinking.)* You surprised me today.
Prosecution	Really?

Defence	You don't usually appear for cases like this. Hardly serious crimes. No national news coverage. You're too expensive for this petty stuff. Why are you involved at all?
Prosecution	As always, to win the case.
Defence	To win your case, or just to make sure I lost mine?
Prosecution	What are you insinuating?
Defence	The establishment's put a lot of effort into this case. A lot of effort that should be going into prosecuting Barabbas.
Prosecution	You haven't heard?
Defence	Heard?
Prosecution	Barabbas was released this morning.
Defence	What! The man's a self confessed bloody murderer.
Prosecution	Public opinion. You heard them shouting his name.
Defence	Since when has public opinion carried any weight in a court of justice.
Prosecution	The establishment cannot afford any trouble at this time.
Defence	And that's why they took you off his case. So why did they put you on mine? Why are they so keen that a terrorist lives and my man dies?
Prosecution	*(Avoiding the issue.)* I've asked for the transcript to be available tomorrow. There are points of law in this case I would like to ...
Defence	Don't play games with me. I've just been party to a miscarriage of justice and I want to know why.

Prosecution	There are precedents being set here.
Defence	He was innocent.
Prosecution	That's beside the point
Defence	And what is the point?
Prosecution	That things stay the way they are.
Defence	But we are the tools of justice.
Prosecution	Justice is what we say it is. Justice is our tool.
Defence	Against an innocent man?
Prosecution	Innocent? Do you know what he's been saying?
Defence	No, tell me. Tell me the words that have got you so scared that you'll send an innocent man to his death.
Prosecution	Never underestimate the power of words. They take root in the people, change their ideas. Change their values.
Defence	For better or worse?
Prosecution	That doesn't matter. It's change. And it's change we have to guard against. You're on dangerous ground. You'd do well to wash your hands of the whole affair. *(Leaves.)*
Defence	Less dangerous than for you, my friend. At least I know I'm wrong. And God I'm sorry. I'm so very, very, sorry.

THE END

The Gardeners

Pruner   *([Ted] has obviously been busy gardening all morning. His back is giving him trouble. He sits down and opens his lunch box.)*

Planter   *([Bert] enters.)* Afternoon Ted.

Pruner   Bert. Have you grown since this morning?

Planter   Don't think so.

Pruner   You look taller to me.

Planter   Ah. I've been muck-spreading.

Pruner   Helps you grow does it?

Planter   No. It sticks to me boots, see. On a good day I can get anything up to six inches stuck to these wellies. *(Sits and starts to pull it off with his fingers.)* What you got then?

Pruner   *(Straightening his back.)* Lumbago.

Planter   On your sandwiches.

Pruner   Oh.

Planter   No, don't tell me. Let me guess. Cheese and pickle.

Pruner   How d'you know that?

Planter   It's Sunday. You've had cheese and pickle sandwiches for lunch every Sunday since we were apprentice gardeners.

Pruner   So I'm a creature of habit. What's wrong with that?

Planter   Nothing.

Pruner	I like cheese and pickle and I like gardening.
Planter	Well you've had thirty-three years of both to find out if you didn't.
Pruner	Thirty-three years.
Planter	Aye. Some of these trees aren't as old as us.
Pruner	I remember planting those olives over there. We probably made this place what it is today. Brought it to fruition you might say.
Planter	You might indeed.
Pruner	Sandwich?
Planter	Don't mind if I do. *(Takes a sandwich with the hand he's just used to pick manure of his wellies. Pulls a face at the taste. Smells the sandwich and then his fingers and slips the sandwich back into Pruner's packet.)* Have you never wanted to do anything else? Other than gardening, I mean.
Pruner	No.
Planter	Never?
Pruner	No.
Planter	What about growing a garden of your own?
Pruner	No. I've always liked this one. Always thought it was something special, like it's got a purpose or something. Of it's very own.
Planter	Hey, up. Here comes Bill. Afternoon, Bill.
Painter	*([Bill] with bucket of whitewash and brushes etc.)* Afternoon Bert, Ted.

Pruner   Bill. Fancy a cheese and pickle sandwich?

Painter   Very kind. *(takes the sandwich Planter has already handled)*

Planter   Ted and me were just having a chat about gardening.

Painter   Well that is unusual.

Planter   Meaning what?

Painter   Meaning your conversation has about as much variation as Ted's Sunday lunch.

Pruner   There's nothing wrong with cheese and pickle and there's nothing wrong with gardening.

Painter   I didn't say there was. *(Bites sandwich.)* I just think there's more to life than both of them. *(Notices strange taste of sandwich.)*

Planter   Oh, that's very rich, coming from the man who spends all day digging graves and whitewashing tombs.

Painter   It's just a question of having a little bit of ambition.

Planter   Which you've got, of course.

Painter   I just think this place could be a bit more than neatly kept graves and cheese and pickle sandwiches.

Planter   Such as what?

Painter   Such as a theme park and hamburgers.

Pruner   Theme park and hamburgers? What are theme parks and hamburgers?

Planter   Well, I know one of them's just an expensive way of getting your innards turned upside down in the company of a lot of noisy kids. But I've never heard of no theme park before.

Pruner   What's a theme park then?

Painter   Well it's a sort of combined fairground and garden. But everything in it has a common theme. Sort of like a focus. I'm going to build one.

Pruner   He's lost me.

Painter   Lots of different ... entertainments, but all with a common thread, like a recurring idea. *(Bites into the sandwich again.)*

Planter   Oh, you mean like the amphitheatre ...

Painter   Is it me or is this cheese off?

Pruner   Amphitheatre?

Planter   Yes, lots of different entertainments. Chariots crashing, gladiators fighting, lions eating people.

Pruner   And what's the recurring idea of the amphitheatre?

Planter   Well, death. Mostly.

Painter   No, my theme park's going to be an unforgettable once in a life time experience.

Planter   Death's a once in a lifetime experience.

Painter   Yes, but it's not constructive is it. I mean, death doesn't make better people.

Pruner   I don't know. I can think of several people I'd like better if they were dead and I never actually had to meet them anymore.

42

Painter	But dead people never get a chance to *use* the experience, do they? They don't get to see life from a new angle.
Pruner	*(Looking heavenward.)* They get to see it from a lot further away.
Planter	And you're going to build a theme park that's going to change people's lives?
Painter	Yes.
Pruner	Isn't that a bit ambitious for a garden?
Painter	Maybe, maybe not.
Pruner	What're you going to call it then, this theme park?
Painter	Garden of Eden: The Paradise Theme Park.
Pruner	Hasn't that been done already?
Painter	Yes, but it didn't last.
Pruner	No and neither will this. If you want my advice you stick to looking after graves. There's a good living in tombs.
Planter	Here, I'd have thought the last place to look for a living *(Laughing)* would be in a tomb.
Pruner	Don't you try and be funny when I'm giving the lad some serious advice. There's a lot of people just dying for a chance to get into graves.
	Bert (Planter) & Bill(Painter) have a laugh together.
	Yes, you go ahead and laugh. But death's the only certain thing in this life and you can't get away from that.

43

Painter	That's what's wrong with this place. It's a monument to death. It's a death theme park.
Planter	Now that's not strictly true. If you want to see a monument to death, you just take a walk into the city. It's full of people who stop living long before they stop breathing. You look at them. No hope, no direction, no vision. And they've as much chance of coming back to life as the corpse in that tomb.
Painter	There isn't a corpse in that tomb.
Planter	Yes there is we put him in there, didn't we, Ted?
Pruner	Yes. Preacher fellow. Crucified on Friday.
Painter	Well he isn't there now.
Planter	Where have the soldiers gone?
Painter	What soldiers?
Planter	The ones guarding the ... how do you know it's empty?
Painter	Cos I've just touched up the whitewash on the inside.
Pruner	Then who helped you move the stone across the entrance?
Painter	It was open. I just walked in. And before you ask me, there was no sign of a forced entry. Least, not from the outside anyway.
Planter	What d'you think, Ted?
Pruner	Don't know. We've never lost a customer before.
Planter	We have now.
Painter	You mean, this morning there's one fewer dead men in the world than there was last night?

44

Planter   That's how it looks.

Pruner   Some people are going to get very upset about this.

Painter   Like who?

Pruner   Well the people who put him there for start.

Planter   And the people who like to believe in certainties.

Painter   How d'you mean?

Planter   Well if death can die, and it looks like it has, maybe even the living can be brought back to life.

Painter   So now there's only one thing you can be certain about.

Planter   What's that?

Painter   Ted's cheese and pickle sandwiches. Come on let's go and have a good look at this tomb. If he really has gone we might have to give this place a new theme. As a monument to life.

Pruner   Aye. I think I'd like that.

THE END

The Fishermen

Followed *(Looking out to sea over the audience.)* There's one there's one ... It's a big one. It's coming this way. Yes! Come on, come on ... you can do it. Oh no ... Too fast, too fast. It's not going to make it. Pull out, pull out, pull out ... Wow! Did you see that? It just smashed to bits on the rocks. So close ... Nothing left. It just ... sprayed itself all over the sand.

Didn't *(Mending a fishing net)* Just like the other fourteen dozen waves you've watched hitting the beach since this morning.

Followed Hey, wave-spotting's a serious business.

Didn't So's mending nets. How about giving some attention to that.

Followed Yeah, okay. Wind's dropping anyway. Waves won't be so good this afternoon.

Didn't I'd have thought you'd have had enough of making waves. You and your friends. You've spent the last three years making waves up and down the country. And look where it's got you; Jesus executed, Judas suicide, Thomas a nervous wreck and Peter a manic depressant. And you back where you started.

Followed Things could be worse.

Didn't *(Look that says 'Oh, yes. And how, precisely?')*

Followed You're right things couldn't be worse. Anyway if things can't get any worse they can only get better. At least, that's what my dad used to say. But then he used to say that the moon went round in circles and if you jumped out of bed fast enough you'd see yourself still lying there. Hey, if we rowed our boat fast enough maybe we'd see Jesus on the shore again. You know, like the first time when he told us to follow him.

Didn't   *Asked* us to follow him. You didn't have to go.

Followed   I couldn't let him go without me.

Didn't   And now you've come back without him. It's a good job one of us kept his feet on the ground or there'd be nothing for you to come back to, now it's all over.

Followed   That's if it is over.

Didn't   What?

Followed   Some of the women say they've seen him. Alive.

Didn't   Well. They would, wouldn't they?

Followed   Why?

Didn't   'Cos they're women, aren't they? They're not like us. They're different.

Followed   There's not much gets past you, is there?

Didn't   I mean emotionally. They miss him. And they can't cope with that so they imagine him. Alive. It's a well known phenomenon.

Followed   Well if Mary imagined him in the garden, how come she didn't recognise him?

Didn't   Maybe she didn't imagine him very clearly.

Followed   What, she imagined him in a false nose and funny glasses?

Didn't   Maybe.

Followed   Nah! She didn't recognise him because he was the last person on earth she expected to see. It was only when she realised he knew her that she realised she knew him.

48

Didn't   *(Not impressed.)* Huh.

Followed   OK, what about Cleopas and ... what's his name walking to
                Emmaus? They can't both have imagined it.

Didn't   A mirage. A trick of the heat on tired eyes. In the desert whole
                regiments have seen the same mirage.

Followed   What, and sat down and had lunch with it? I don't think so.

Didn't   Still a bit iffy if you ask me.

Followed   You're worse than Thomas. Do you want a personal appearance as
                well?

Didn't   That was just a ghost. An apparition.

Followed   Then why did it invite Thomas to touch him? Even offered him the
                nail holes in his hands. That was a man. As solid as ... *(Picks up a
                rock)* this rock. *(Hits Didn't on the head with it.)*

Didn't   Ow! So it was a walking corpse. A temporarily revived body.
                Magicians, illusionists do it all the time.

Followed   Alright then, what about yesterday? Just down the beach. Peter and
                the lads. Fishing all night. Caught nothing. A stranger appears and
                tells them where to fish. Nearly sinks the boat they catch so many.
                Back on the beach, it's Jesus, isn't it? Again! He cooks them
                breakfast and eats it with them. A walking corpse wouldn't eat
                barbequed fish.

Didn't   Then it was someone else.

Followed   Who, then. Who could it be? His twin? His stunt double?

Didn't   I don't know, maybe it was an angel.

49

Followed	Rubbish. That was no angel, it was Jesus himself. And you know it, you just won't admit it.
Didn't	Well what about you, have you seen him?
Followed	No. No, I haven't.
Didn't	Then how can you believe them? Mary and the others. How do you know?
Followed	Because I know them. Because I knew him. I won't be the only one who believes without seeing.
Didn't	You just won't listen to reason, will you?
Followed	Look, better men than me will put up better arguments than you. And when all's done, they'll find there's no other explanation.
Didn't	There's always another explanation.
Followed	What, one they'll believe with such conviction that they'll die rather than give themselves to anything less?
Didn't	No, just one that fits the facts.
Followed	Look, the facts are: One, the tomb is empty. Two, the body's gone. Three, People are seeing him alive and risking their lives telling about it. And four, you'll believe any half baked story just to avoid having to admit the truth.
Didn't	And what if it is the truth? What if he is alive? What difference does it make?
Followed	Who to? You or to me?
Didn't	To me.
Followed	None at all.

Didn't   How do you know?

Followed   Because to you, he was never alive in the first place.

Didn't   Yes he was. I saw him here, the day you and the others went off with him.

Followed   No. You didn't see him. What you saw might as well have been a corpse already for all it mattered to you. If he was nothing to you then, how can he be anything to you now?

Didn't   He never told us who he was then. Or where he was going. He just said 'follow me' and went. What was I supposed to do?

Followed   It was a simple enough choice.

Didn't   But he never gave us any details. Never told us what to expect. And he certainly never mentioned rising from the dead.

Followed   Would you have believed him?

Didn't   No.

Followed   So what's the difference?

Didn't   The difference is ... the difference is ... Oh what's the point.

Followed   The point is he didn't try to make it difficult for us. You're doing that for yourself. He didn't ask you to believe, or doubt or understand or anything. He only asked you to follow. Because that was all you needed to do for the time being.

Didn't   But I didn't know where to.

Followed   You didn't need to, You weren't leading.

Didn't   So I missed him, then.

Followed   First time, yes.

Didn't   First time? You mean I get a second chance?

Followed   He wouldn't come back from the dead if he didn't offer a good line in second chances.

Didn't   Wouldn't it be a bit like backing the winner after you know the final score?

Followed   Better than backing the loser when you know the game's lost.

Didn't   So where do we go from here?

Followed   Like I said, we're not leading.

THE END

The Angels

Junior *(Satisfied at the apparently simplistic happy ending.)* So. There you are then.

Senior There you are what?

Junior I told you so.

Senior Told me what?

Junior That everything would turn out alright in the end.

Senior Would you mind telling me what you're talking about?

Junior Jesus. Everything's alright again. Mind you, he had me worried. For a moment there I didn't think he was going to make it. But now he's back and everything's like it was before.

Senior Like it was before?

Junior Yes. Or better.

Senior I don't think Judas would see it that way.

Junior Yes, well, the baddies have to get it in the end, don't they? It's all part of the happy ending.

Senior And that's all you think this is? A happy ending added onto a tragic story?

Junior It's got to have a happy ending.

Senior Why?

Junior It makes people feel well, nice.

Senior   I should think Peter feels anything but nice at the moment.

Junior   He shouldn't have let Jesus down like that. Disowning him in public. And not just once either. Then letting him die without a word of protest.

Senior   Even so. I don't think having Jesus around to remind him of the fact will make him feel any better. And then there's Pilate and the religious leaders. This isn't a happy ending for them, it's their worst nightmare.

Junior   Well no, but it's the ending everyone else expected.

Senior   How could they know what to expect? There must have been a hundred possible endings. Why this one?

Junior   Because it's the only ending that makes sense. The story was leading up to this all the time.

Senior   I see. So even from the beginning you knew how it was going to end.

Junior   We're angels. We're eternal beings we can see the beginning and end of everything.

Senior   Precisely. And from that privileged position you're trying to explain the ending in the light of the story.

Junior   Look, I'm sorry but I haven't the faintest ...

Senior   When you're not on duty what do you do?

Junior   Praise. Sing. Read.

Senior   You read. And what do you read?

Junior   Stories. Adventures. Thrillers mostly.

Senior	Thrillers?

Junior Yes, like detective stories, mysteries.

Senior As do the mortals. And do they all have happy endings?

Junior Not always.

Senior Well do they always have the ending you would expect?

Junior Oh, no. In the best ones, the ending's a complete surprise. Sometimes you never know how it's going to turn out 'til the last page.

Senior How can the ending be a surprise? Surely if you read the story, and understood it, the ending would be exactly what the story led you to expect.

Junior Oh, no, you can't understand the whole story 'til you get to the end. It doesn't make sense until you know how it all ends. Then you realise how all the bits of the story fit together, and find out what was really going on.

Senior Exactly. A denouement.

Junior Pardon?

Senior An unknotting. An unravelling of the uncertainties and confusions of the plot. It's the ending that explains the story and not the other way 'round.

Junior So you're saying it's the ending, the resurrection, that makes sense of the life of Jesus.

Senior It explains what was really going on. That God himself was at work as a mortal man. The resurrection is not an addition to the story, it is it's resolution.

Junior   And it really was a complete surprise to them?

Senior   As wholly unexpected as the light of creation. But ... that will never happen again. From now on even mortals will have an angel's view of the story, and they too will know the ending from the beginning.

Junior   Won't that spoil the surprise for them?

Senior   Yes. Yes, I think it will. But there is a greater surprise waiting for each of them.

Junior   What could be more surprising than a living God?

Senior   Meeting him. Shall we go?

Junior   Go where?

Senior   To open the gates of course.

Junior   Open the gates of Heaven? Who for?

Senior   Anyone who wants to come in.

Junior   What, anyone?

Senior   From now on, yes.

Junior   Wow!

Senior   Yes. I thought that might surprise you.

THE END